Teachers' Guide

Year 1

Story-wri[illegible]ng

Sc[illegible]

Written by
Frances Mackay

HOPSCOTCH
EDUCATIONAL PUBLISHING

Published by Hopscotch
A division of MA Education Ltd
St Jude's Church, Dulwich Road
Herne Hill, London SE24 0PB
Tel: 020 7738 5454

Written by Frances Mackay
Series design by Blade Communications
Illustrated by Debbie Clark
Cover illustrated by Kirsty Wilson
Printed in the UK by CLE, St Ives, Huntingdon, Cambridgeshire

ISBN 1-905390-26-2
ISBN 978-1-905390-26-7

Year 1

Story-writing
SCAFFOLDS

CONTENTS

Story-writing Scaffolds for Year 1

INTRODUCTION

Story-writing Scaffolds Year 1 is intended for use in schools to help teach children how to write effective short stories in a variety of different genres. It aims to improve the children's ability to organise their own writing. As they work through the units, they assemble a portfolio of stories containing genre-specific vocabulary and writing features. The chosen text types correspond to those in the National Literacy Strategy's *Framework for teaching*.

The book is accompanied by six full colour fiction titles that are used in conjunction with each unit in the book. The six exemplar storybooks are:

- *Making Lunch* by Jenny Feely;
- *Sebastian* by Sarah Prince;
- *Goldilocks and the Three Bears* retold by Jenny Feely;
- *The Picnic* retold by Jenny Feely;
- *Annie and the Pirates* by Jenny Feely;
- *Lizard's Tail* by Mark Gagiero.

(The six books are all part of the 'Alphakids' series published by Eleanor Curtain Publishing.)

Contents
The book contains six units – two for each term. Each unit contains:

- notes for teachers about each genre;
- guidance for teachers on the questions to ask and discussion ideas after reading the exemplar storybook;
- three photocopiable activity sheets to follow up the reading of the story;
- a wealth of further speaking and listening and writing ideas to carry out after reading the story;
- photocopiable differentiated story scaffolds;
- photocopiable differentiated word banks.

How to use the units in this book

1. Share the exemplar storybook with the children. The guidance notes for each unit provide suggestions for questions to ask the children after/during the reading. The notes also provide ideas for further discussion.
2. Use the three photocopiable activity pages for each unit to revisit the story with the children. These pages include comprehension, sequencing, grammar and punctuation activities. These pages may also provide you with ideas for developing your own activities.
3. If appropriate, select some activities from the further ideas section. There are enough ideas on these pages to carry out related work for several weeks.
4. Tell the children they are going to write their own story. Provide them with either Scaffold 1 or Scaffold 2 depending on their level of ability/experience. For Scaffold 2 it is important that you have made up the booklet (see below) before giving it to the children to work on. You can also provide them with a copy of the related word bank provided to help them with their writing.

How to use the scaffolds
Scaffold 1
This scaffold is intended for younger/less experienced children. Most of the story has been completed for them – they are required to think of an appropriate ending. An adult will need to read the instructions to the child and discuss ideas with them about how the story could develop. The adult could scribe the story for the child. The word bank can be used to support independent writing.

Scaffold 2
This scaffold is intended for older/more experienced children. When cut out and assembled it becomes a little storybook that the child can complete and keep. It will take a little organising for the adult – but it is well worth it when the book is completed!

How to make the storybook

1. Photocopy the required pages.
2. Cut around the page outlines.

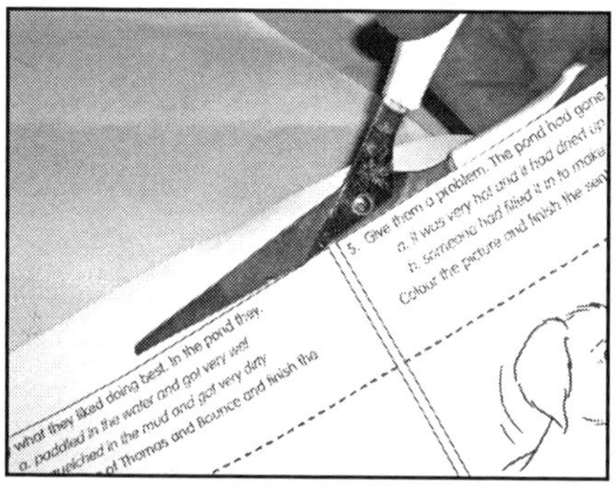

3. Glue the page with instructions 8 and 1 back to back with the page of instructions 2 and 7. (Or use a photocopier that prints on both sides.)

Do the same with the pages of instructions 6 and 3 and 4 and 5.

4. Fold the pages to make the book, ensuring the numbered instructions are in the correct order. Then sew or staple the pages in the centre (below the dotted line only).

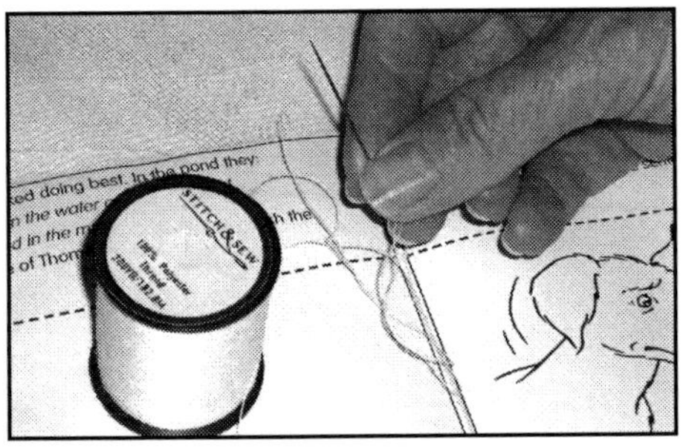

5. The book is now ready for the children to use. An adult can help them to read the instructions at the top of each page. The children draw and write the story. Note: the choices provided at the top of each page are guidelines only. The children may prefer to use their own ideas.

6. Once the book has been completed, the instructions should be cut off.

Links to the National Literacy framework for Year 1

Unit 1 – Family life stories

Genre: Stories about familiar settings

Photocopiable activities:
page 8 – story sequencing
page 9 – the term 'sentence' (Term 1: S6, S7)
page 10 – rhyming words (Term 1: W5)

Unit 2 – School life stories

Genre: Stories about familiar settings

Photocopiable activities:
page 22 – story sequencing
page 23 – capital letters and full stops (Term 1: S8)
page 24 – writing captions (Term 1: T14)

Unit 3 – Traditional tales

Genre: Traditional stories and rhymes

Photocopiable activities:
page 36 – story sequencing
page 37 – forming sentences (Term 2: S6)
page 38 – plurals (Term 2: W8)

Unit 4 – Playscripts

Genre: Plays

Photocopiable activities:
page 50 – story sequencing
page 51 – capital letters and full stops (Term 2: S5, S6, S7)
page 52 – rhyming words (Term 2: W3)

Unit 5 – Fantasy stories

Genre: Fantasy

Photocopiable activities:
page 64 – story sequencing
page 65 – words linked to a topic (Term 3: W8)
page 66 – verbs with 'ed' (Term 3: W6)

Unit 6 – Animal stories

Genre: Animals

Photocopiable activities:
page 78 – story sequencing
page 79 – question marks (Term 3: S7)
page 80 – capitals for names (Term 3: S5)

Unit 1

Family life stories

Stories about family life are very popular. Children are immediately able to identify with the setting even if the family types and experiences don't quite match their own.

Family stories can be about all kinds of families and family situations:

- Siblings – *Titch* by Pat Hutchins – about being the smallest and youngest in the family;
- New family members – *Sophie and the New Baby* by Catherine and Laurence Anholt – about the changes that occur when a new baby arrives;
- Relationships – *Granpa* by John Burningham – about children sharing experiences with grandparents;
- Fears and worries – *Where's My Mum?* by Leon Rosselson – about a child's feelings of insecurity;
- Lifestyles – *Happy Families* series by Janet and Allan Ahlberg – about different occupations and family lifestyles;
- Biracial – *An African Princess* by Lyra Edmonds – about an Afro-American girl;
- Adoption – *We Wanted You* by Liz Rosenberg – about international adoption.

Family stories often have a dominant character in them, such as a very busy mother, an adventurous grandfather or an annoying sister. In such stories, the tale is usually told from the viewpoint of a member of the family who bears the brunt of these characters' behaviour. The writer does this to help the reader develop empathy with the character – most of us, after all, have similar people in our own families.

Apart from picture books intended to help children identify with themselves and their family situations, few family life stories are written exclusively about the everyday lives of the family – perhaps this would be too boring for the reader! Most family stories therefore also contain elements of other genres such as mystery, adventure or fantasy.

Family stories usually have a happy ending.

Scaffold 1: Sunil's story (page 12)
Ideas for what happened could include Sunil phoning for an ambulance or the doctor, or finding a bandage and helping his dad to put it round his leg. Discuss with the children whether the story ends in a day out (the title) or not.

Family life stories

Examples of family life stories

No Matter What by Debi Gliori (Bloomsbury, 2003)

It's Not Fair by Bel Mooney (Egmont Books, 2002)

So Much by Trish Cooke (Walker Books, 1996)

I'm a Big Sister by Joanna Cole (William Morrow, 1997)

Grandad Pot by Siobhan Dodds (Walker Books, 2003)

My Brother Sammy by Becky Edwards (Bloomsbury, 2000)

My Mum by Anthony Browne (Doubleday, 2005)

My Dad by Anthony Browne (Doubleday, 2003)

When Mum Turned into a Monster by Joanna Harrison (Picture Lions, 1996)

Daddy's Lullaby by Tony Bradman (Bloomsbury, 2002)

Making Lunch

by Jenny Feely

Questions to ask and discussion ideas

Front cover
Read the title and the author's and illustrator's names. Ask the children to tell you what the story might be about. Do they think it might be a happy story, for example? What kind of lunch might they be making? (What can they tell from the picture?) Do they like the cover? Why/why not?

Who might the man be? Who might the girl be? What is the man doing? What is the girl doing? Do they look happy or sad? What tells you this? Are they inside or outside?

Pages 2 and 3
What is Uncle Vin doing? What kind of soup might it be? Who has soup for lunch sometimes? What is your favourite soup? Have you ever helped to make soup? How is it made?

What is Sam doing? Should he be doing that inside the house? What might happen? How old do you think Sam is?

What does Uncle Vin ask? What does Sam reply? Why do you think he says this?

What can you see in the picture? What room are they in?

Pages 4 and 5
What is Uncle Vin doing? Where is he? What has he got in his hand? What does he say? Why do you think he has come into this room?

What kind of sandwich do you think he might be making? Who has sandwiches for lunch? Who has made a sandwich? What is your favourite kind of sandwich? Why?

Who else is in the room? What is she doing?

What does Uncle Vin ask? What does Anna reply? Why do you think she says this?

Pages 6 and 7
What is Uncle Vin doing? Where is he? What has he got in his hands? What does he say?

Have you ever made juice from squeezing fruit? What does it taste like? How else can you get fruit juice? What kinds of fruit juice do you like?

What does Uncle Vin ask?

Who else is in the room? What is he carrying? Why do you think he might need this? Who is with him? What might his/her name be?

What does Sam reply? Why do you think he says this?

What else can you see in the room?

Pages 8 and 9
What is Uncle Vin doing? Where is he? What kind of fruit might be in the salad? Who has eaten fruit salad? What was in it? How do you make it? What fruit can you see on the table? Who likes fruit salad?

Who else is in the room? What is she doing?

What does Uncle Vin ask? What does Anna reply?

Where have you seen this picture before?

Pages 10 and 11
What is Uncle Vin doing? Where is he? What can you see on the table?

Who else is in the room? What are they doing? What do they ask Uncle Vin? What do you think Uncle Vin will say?

Pages 12 and 13
What does Uncle Vin reply? What had he asked the children to help him with? What had they replied?

Look at the picture of Sam and Anna. What do you think they are feeling? How do they look?

Pages 14 and 15
What is Uncle Vin doing? What did he say? How do Sam and Anna look? What do you think they are thinking?

Page 16
What are Sam and Anna doing? Why do you think they are doing this? How do you think they feel now? How do you think Uncle Vin felt when they wouldn't help him? How do you think he feels now? Do you think they might be willing to help more in the future? Do you help at home? What kinds of things do you do?

Name

Cut out the pictures.
Put them in order to tell the story of 'Making Lunch'.

Name

Use the words in the box to complete these sentences.

have	making	who	help
said	too	busy	me

1. 'I'm ________________ soup,' said Uncle Vin.
2. '____________ will help me?'

3. 'Not me,' __________ Sam.
4. 'I'm too ____________.'
5. 'I'm making sandwiches,' ___________ Uncle Vin.
6. 'Who will _____________ me?'

7. 'Not _______,' said Anna.
8. 'I'm __________ busy.'
9. 'Can we ____________ lunch now?'
10. 'No, you are too ____________ to eat lunch.'

Write a sentence of your own using some of these words.

____

Name

Choose the words that rhyme. Write them in the pots.

fed	me
help	bed
shed	busy
soup	making
who	Ted
bread	will
uncle	can
lunch	head

make	come
do	have
help	busy
new	ball
table	zoo
blue	pot
lunch	chew
Sam	you

Further activity ideas

Speaking and listening

- Ask the children to recall what Uncle Vin made for the children's lunch. List the items on the board. Ask them to tell you about their favourite types of soup, sandwiches, drinks and desserts.

- Ask the children to carry out a lunch survey of other children in the school. What foods are lunch favourites? Ask them to present their results to the rest of the class.

- Dramatise the story with the children acting the parts of Uncle Vin, Sam and Anna. Discuss the way each character might talk and how their expressions might change during different parts of the story. For example, how might the children's faces look when Uncle Vin tells them they can't have any lunch?

- The children could interview the school cook or local restaurant chef. They could use a tape recorder to record the interview and report back to the class. Things to explore could include finding out about healthy and not so healthy foods, how to prepare food safely, how menus are decided and so on.

- Ask the children to recall events with their family. Do they have an uncle? What sorts of things do they do with him? What other family members can there be? Share anecdotes about funny/favourite days with family members.

- Ask the children to interview members of their family to find out about their lives/past experiences. Good questions to ask include:
  - *What was the house like that you lived in as a child?*
  - *What was your bedroom like as a child?*
  - *What was your favourite place to visit as a child?*
  - *What was your favourite lunch as a child?*
  - *Where did you go to school? What was in the classrooms?*
  - *What did you do for fun?*
  - *What hobbies did you have?*
  - *Where did you go when you wanted to hide?*
  - *Did your family ever move?*
  - *When did you get married? What was your house like then?*
  - *Who lived in your house with you as a child?*
  - *Who was your best friend? What was he/she like?*
  - *What were your neighbours like?*
  - *How did you travel from place to place?*
  - *What did you do for holidays?*
  - *What was your first job?*
  - *Did anyone in the family have something unusual happen to them?*

Writing

- Ask the children to draw or use clay to make models of the things Uncle Vin made for lunch. They could write captions to label each item or write sentences. They could then draw and write about their own favourite lunches.

- Ask the children to write another episode to the story. What happens the next day? Perhaps the children decide to make lunch for Uncle Vin – what happens?

- Ask the children to make lists of foods suitable for lunches. They could each be assigned different letters of the alphabet. Make the lists into a word wall or make an alphabetical display of words. The words could be presented in the shape of the food item.

- Find out about healthy eating. Design and make healthy lunch menus.

- Ask the children to write about something they did with their uncle/auntie/grandfather/grandmother.

- Read other stories about lunches, such as *The Lighthouse Keeper's Lunch* by David and Ronda Armitage. Write stories about lunches/food. Make a class book or make individual books in the shape of foods.

- Make up sandwich recipes – they could be real or fantasy ones, such as a sandwich for a dragon or a monster.

- Arrange for the children to make their own lunches at school. Ask them to write out the recipes and share them with others by making a class lunch cookbook.

- Write other stories with catchphrases like 'Not me, I'm too busy,' such as: 'Not me, I'm not brave enough,'; 'Not me, I'm too old,' or 'Not me, I'm too little.'

Unit 1 – Scaffold 1

Sunil's Day Out by ____________________

1. Colour the picture.

Sunil is five years old.

2. Colour the picture.

This is Sunil's dad.

3. Colour the picture.

Dad told Sunil he would take him to the park.
Sunil ran to get his coat.

4. Colour the picture.

When Sunil came back, his dad was on the floor.
He had hurt his leg.

5. Draw and write what happens in the end.

Sunil's Day Out
Word bank

bandage
carried
carry
coat
dad
doctor
down
floor
happy
helped
him
hurt
leg
outside
park
phone
ran
room
sore
stick
Sunil
take
up
very
walk

My own words

8. Finish the book blurb.

This story is about a family. In the family were ____________________ and ____________________.

One day ____________ came to stay. She brought ____________________ with her. She made a lot of noise.

Read the story to find out what happened.

Unit 1 – Scaffold 2

1. This is the cover of your book. Colour it and write your name.

Gran's visit

by ____________________

2. You are going to write a story about a family.
Choose who is in the family:
   a. Mum, Dad, Robbie and Kate Lewis
   b. Mum and Khan Dhesi
Draw the family and finish the sentence.

The ____________ family had some news. Gran was coming to visit them.

7. Say how the story ends.
Everyone was very happy.
   a. Gran made lots of new friends.
   b. Gran won first prize in a competition.
Colour the picture and finish the sentences.

Gran liked her new hobby. The family was __________. The neighbours were __________. Gran ________________ ______________________________.

6. Say how the problem was solved.

The family found something else for Gran to do. It was:

a. rollerblading

b. kite flying

Draw Gran doing her new hobby. Finish the sentences.

The family found something else for ___________ to do. They showed her how to ______________________________ .

3. Choose a good beginning.

a. Everyone was very happy. Gran was lots of fun.

b. Everyone was unhappy. Gran was often grumpy.

Colour the picture and finish the sentences.

Everyone was ____________________. Gran could be __________________________.
The family waited at the train station for her to arrive.

4. Say what happened next.

Gran brought a big box with her. Inside the box was:

a. a drum kit

b. a lot of music CDs

Colour the picture and finish the sentences.

When ______________ arrived, she had a big box with her. She said it had ___________________________ inside it!

5. Give the family a problem.

Gran said she wanted to:

a. play the drums very loudly every day

b. sing along to her CDs every day

Colour the picture and finish the sentences.

Every day Gran ________________________ ________________________.

The family was _________________. The neighbours were _________________.

Gran's visit
Word bank

arrive	happy	problem
competition	hobby	rollerblading
drum kit	inside	singing
enjoyed	kite flying	something else
excited	loudly	train station
family	music	unhappy
first	neighbours	very
friends	new	visit
fun	playing	waving
gran	prize	

My own words

Unit 2

School life stories

Stories about school life often deal with issues such as bullying, friendship, growing up, peer pressure and relationships between staff and pupils. All this is set against the background of the everyday school routine.

Most stories about school life provide children with settings and scenarios that are immediately recognisable and familiar to the reader (for example, *Jennifer Jones Won't Leave Me Alone* by Frieda Wishinsky).

Such stories enable the reader to empathise with the characters and appreciate the things the characters are experiencing.

Other school stories, however, use the familiar school setting but introduce characters and situations that are clearly based on fantasy (for example, *I Hate School* by Jeanne Willis).

These stories enable the reader to let their imagination go wild and to fantasise about what school COULD be like!

Many school stories have the 'good' teacher who is understanding and kind as well as the 'bad' teacher who takes little interest in the children and is stern and forbidding. The stories usually also have a character who is a 'model' pupil as well as a character who is always in trouble. Little is known about any of the characters' lives outside the school environment. School stories for very young children are often written to reassure the readers. Common themes are: first day at school, not wanting to go to school, new teachers and making friends.

School life stories

Examples of school life stories

Little Rabbit Goes to School by Harry Horse (Penguin, 2005)

I Hate School by Jeanne Willis (Andersen Press, 2005)

There's a Dragon at My School by Jenny Hawthorn and Tyler (Usborne, 2004)

Owl at School by Helen Nicoll (Puffin, 2002)

I Am Too Absolutely Small for School by Lauren Child (Orchard Books, 2003)

Laura's Star and the New Teacher by Klaus Baumgart (Little Tiger Press, 2004)

Jennifer Jones Won't Leave Me Alone by Frieda Wishinsky (Random House, 2003)

Cleversticks by Bernard Ashley (Picture Lions, 2002)

Starting School by Janet and Allan Ahlberg (Puffin, 1990)

Lucy and Tom Go to School by Shirley Hughes (Puffin, 1992)

Once Upon an Ordinary School Day by Colin McNaughton (Andersen Press, 2005)

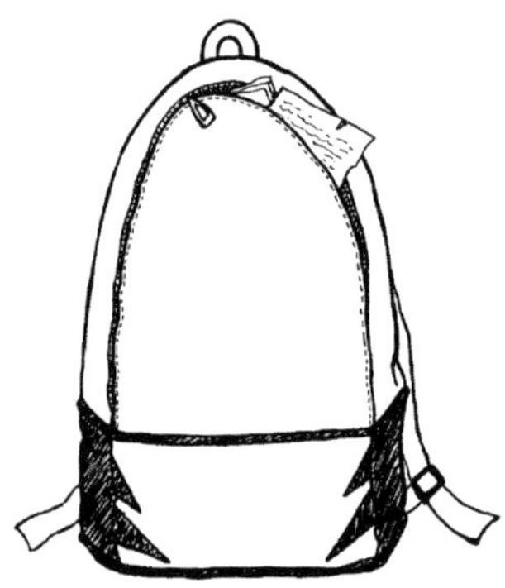

Sebastian

by Sarah Prince

Questions to ask and discussion ideas

Front cover
Read the title and the author's and illustrator's names. Ask the children to tell you what the story might be about. Who is Sebastian? What kind of creature is he?

What do you think he is sitting on?

Pages 2 and 3
What is Sebastian doing? Where do you think he might be? What can you see in the picture?

Is Sebastian clever? Can he do lots of different things? Does he know lots of things? What kinds of things do you think he might know/be able to do?

What does Sebastian not like doing? Why do you think he doesn't like going to school?

Pages 4 and 5
What does Sebastian's mother say to him every morning? Where is Sebastian's mother when she says this? Where is Sebastian? What does he do?

Do you ever feel like not getting out of bed? What do your parents do to get you out of bed?

Look at the picture on page 5. What does Sebastian's mother do?

Pages 6 and 7
What does Sebastian's mother say every morning? What does Sebastian do?

Where is Sebastian? What was he doing before he hid under the table? What is Sebastian's mother doing?

Do you clean your teeth every morning? What do you have for breakfast?

Pages 8 and 9
What does Sebastian's mother say to him every morning? What does Sebastian do?

Why do you think he does this every day?

Look at page 9. What are Sebastian and his mother doing? Do you think they have far to go to school? Why/why not?

Pages 10 and 11
What does Sebastian's teacher say to him every morning? What would Sebastian feel like doing? What can you see in the picture? Where is Sebastian?

Why do you think he feels like crying? Have you ever felt like crying at school? What made you feel better?

Page 12
What does Sebastian's teacher ask him to do? What would Sebastian feel like doing instead?

What are all the other birds doing? Do you like reading books at school? Which is your favourite?

Why do you think Sebastian doesn't want to read?

Page 13
What does Sebastian's teacher ask him to do? What does Sebastian feel like doing?

Pages 14 and 15
What happens one day when Sebastian feels like crying? Who helps him? What does she say?

What does Sebastian do? How does he feel?

How important is it to have friends at school? How do friends help you at school? Have you ever made a new friend at school? How did you make them feel happy?

Page 16
Look at the picture. What is Sebastian doing? Why do you think he likes to go to school now?

What did Sebastian do before when his mother tried to get him to go to school? What do you think he does now?

Name

Cut out the pictures.

Put them in order to tell the story of 'Sebastian'.

Name

Rewrite these sentences, using capital letters and full stops.

1. sebastian did not like going to school

____

2. every morning Sebastian would hide under the table

____

3. every morning Sebastian would hide behind the door

____

4. come and read a book

____

5. sebastian would feel like crying

____

6. one day Isabella asked Sebastian to play with her

____

7. he was very happy

____

8. sebastian likes to go to school

____

On the back draw Sebastian and write a sentence about him.

Name

Choose words from the box to label each picture.

cry	school	sing	door	table	book

Draw a picture from the story about Sebastian and label it.

Further activity ideas

Speaking and listening

- ❑ Ask the children to tell you what Sebastian used to do every morning before he went to school. Ask them to tell you the things they do before they come to school each morning.

- ❑ Dramatise the story with the children acting the parts of Sebastian, Sebastian's mother, Sebastian's teacher, Sebastian's classmates and Isabella.

- ❑ Ask the children to tell you things they could do to help someone who is unhappy at school. Make a list and put it on the classroom wall. Refer to it whenever someone is unhappy – read out the ideas to find something that will help.

- ❑ Ask the children to recall their first days at school. How did they feel? What kinds of things did they do? What did they like? What didn't they like? They could ask their parents/carers about their first days at school – what can they remember? Ask the children to share these memories (including your own!) with the rest of the class.

- ❑ Ask the children to interview their family members about their experiences at school. What do they remember? What was it like then? Suitable questions to ask include:
  - *Where did you go to school?*
  - *How did you get to school?*
  - *What things did you see on the way?*
  - *What was it like there?*
  - *What was the building like?*
  - *What kinds of things were in the classroom?*
  - *What were your favourite things at school?*
  - *What didn't you like at school?*
  - *Who was your best friend? What was he/she like?*
  - *What did you do at playtime?*
  - *What subjects did you do in school?*
  - *What rules can you remember?*
  - *What happened when you broke the rules?*

- ❑ Ask the children to bring in photographs taken at school. They could be of themselves or other family members. Ask the children to tell the others about their photograph – who is in it, what is happening and why they chose this photo.

- ❑ Share other stories about school. Ask the children to sit with a friend and tell them what would make their school a perfect place to be at!

Writing

- ❑ Ask the children to draw and write about what Sebastian did before he went to school and what he did at school. They could then draw and write about the things they do before and at school.

- ❑ Ask the children to write another episode to the story. What happens the next day? What does Sebastian do when his mother says: 'Time to get up, Sebastian,', 'Time to clean your teeth, Sebastian,' and 'Time for school, Sebastian.'? What does he do at school?

- ❑ Ask the children to make lists of things they like doing at school. You could use the lists as checklists for individual rewards for good behaviour or work!

- ❑ Find out about schools in the past. Make a class book – 'Schools then and now'. Include photographs, writing and drawings.

- ❑ Ask the children to write about their own school. Make a class book. The book could be used to help new children who come into the classroom during the year.

- ❑ Write stories about school: 'The day my teacher disappeared!', 'The school dinner disaster' or 'The playground monster'.

- ❑ Make a school ABC. Ask the children to find words to do with school. Put the words on a word wall or clothes line so they can refer to them in their writing.

- ❑ Rewrite the ending to 'Sebastian'. Reread the story up to page 14 – 'One day when Sebastian felt like crying...' Ask the children to write their own ending.

- ❑ Use a digital camera to take photographs around the school. Ask the children to write captions or sentences for each one. Make a display in the school's entrance area.

Tom and Sam by ____________________________

1. Colour the picture.

This is Tom. He is 5 years old.

2. Colour the picture.

This is Tom's brother, Sam.
He is 10 years old.

3. Colour the picture.

Tom and Sam walk to school together.
But at school Sam will not let Tom play with him.

4. Colour the picture.

One day, Tom hid Sam's football.

5. Draw and write what Sam does.

6. Finish the story. Draw and write what happens in the end.

Tom and Sam
Word bank

again
all
break
brother
day
every
family
football
friends
games
good
happy
help
him
his
lunch
match
play
played
playing
sad
school
together
walk
win

My own words

8. Finish the book blurb.

This story is about a boy called ________ who took a ______________ to school on his first day!

Read the story to find out what happened.

Unit 2 – Scaffold 2

1. This is the cover of your book.
Colour it and write your name.

First day at school

by ____________________

2. You are going to write a story about a new boy who comes to school. Choose who this new boy is:

   a. Tim

   b. Peter

Draw the boy on the page below. Finish the sentence.

Today was the first day at school for _____________. He did not want to go so he took something from home with him to make him feel better.

7. Say how the story ends.

Everyone liked the new boy so they:

   a. made sure they played with him at lunchtime

   b. took it in turns to look after the pet

Colour the picture and finish the sentences.

Everyone liked _____________ so they

____

_____________________________________.

__________ decided he would never take a pet to ____________ again!

6. Say how the problem was solved.

a. The children chased the pet until they caught it.

b. The children made a safe trap to catch it.

Draw the children catching the pet. finish the sentences.

The children were very clever. They

______________________________ .

Soon the ____________ was caught.

Everyone was very ____________ .

3. Choose a good beginning.

a. The children were excited.

b. The children were worried.

Colour the picture and finish the sentence.

Everyone in Mrs Wilson's class was very

_______________ when they heard that

a new boy was going to be in the class.

4. Say what happened next.

When the door opened, the new boy was carrying:

a. a pet mouse in a cage

b. a pet dog on a lead

Draw the pet. Finish the sentences.

When ______________ came in, he had

a ______________________________.

Mrs Wilson was not very happy but she found a place for ______________ to put the pet.

5. Give the class a problem. The pet got out and:

a. ate the children's lunches

b. tipped all the paints over the floor

Colour the picture and finish the sentence.

Before lunch the ____________ got out and ______________________________

______________________________.

First day at school
Word bank

after	escaped	person
ate	everyone	pet
better	excited	played
cage	first	really
carrying	floor	safe
catch	happy	sorry
caught	lunches	terrible
chased	made	tipped
class	mouse	want
clever	new	worried
dog	paints	

My own words

Unit 3

Traditional tales

Traditional tales are stories that have been passed on as spoken tales from one generation to the next. They have been told and retold, sometimes with subtle changes woven into the story by the narrator. These stories were eventually written down in their many forms. The genre encompasses several types of story, including fairy tales, folk tales, myths, legends and fables. Many of the themes of traditional tales appear across different cultures and numerous versions exist of each one. This is due to the origins of traditional tales being spoken as opposed to being recorded in a written form.

Fairy tales encompass an element of magic or enchantment; for example, a prince turning into a frog in 'The Golden Ball', a pumpkin turned into a coach by a fairy godmother in 'Cinderella' and the magic beans that grow into a gigantic beanstalk in 'Jack and the Beanstalk'. Fairy tales often begin with 'Once upon a time ...' and usually end with everyone living happily ever after. Sometimes these stories also contain magical folk such as fairies or elves; for example, 'The Elves and the Shoemaker'.

Folk tales originate from a particular ethnic people and the oral tradition of these tales tells the story of their history, culture and superstitions. Animals frequently feature in folk tales, alongside or instead of humans, both of whom succeed or fail in response to their ability to be quick-witted.

Myths are explanation stories which explain the origins of natural and supernatural phenomena.

Legends usually refer to individual characters, great heroes or kings who lived in the periods before written records. While based on truth, they have often been exaggerated over time.

Fables often feature a talking animal as the main character. This type of traditional tale teaches the reader a moral or lesson to be learned from their behaviour or actions. The most famous fables are those of Aesop, who is thought to have been a Greek slave who lived about 600BC.

Scaffold 1
You may need to suggest to the children a possible scenario for escaping the clutches of the cat: for example, the mice grant the cat three wishes if he promises not to eat them or they use magic to turn him into ... (stone, a spider, food and so on).

Traditional tales

Examples of traditional tales

The Very Best of Aesop's Fables by Margaret Clark (Walker Books, 1996)

A First Book of Fairy Tales retold by Mary Hoffman (Dorling Kindersley, 2001)

Snow White and the Seven Dwarfs retold by Jenny Koralek (Macdonald Young Books, 1997)

The Nursery Storybook by Georgie Adams (Orion Children's Books, 1998)

Bedtime Stories – 4 well-loved fairy tales to read aloud and share by Beth Harwood (Silver Dolphin, 2005)

The Princess and the Pea by Lauren Child (Puffin, 2005)

Beauty and the Beast by Maria Mantovani (Mercury Books, 2005)

Goldilocks and the Three Bears

retold by Jenny Feely

Questions to ask and discussion ideas

Front cover
Read the title and the author's and illustrator's names. Ask the children to tell you if they have heard of this story before. Do any of them have a copy of this story at home?

Tell the children that the story is a traditional tale. Do they know what kind of story this is? What sorts of things usually happen in traditional tales?

Ask them to look at the cover. What can they see?

Pages 2 and 3
What are the names of the three bears? What do they love to eat? What was wrong with their porridge? What did they decide to do?

What can you see in the picture? What is on the table? What are the bears wearing?

Pages 4 and 5
Who was out walking in the woods? What did she do when she saw the bears' house?

Whose porridge did she try first? What did she say? Whose porridge did she try next? What did she say? Whose porridge did she try last? What did she say? What did she do?

What can you see in the picture? What is Goldilocks wearing? Why do you think she is called Goldilocks? What kind of cottage do the bears live in? Why do you think there is a jug upside down on the fence? What do you think it might be used for? (Fetching water from the well?)

Pages 6 and 7
Whose chair did Goldilocks sit on first? What did she say? Whose chair did she sit on next? What did she say? Whose chair did she sit on last? What did she say? What happened? Why do you think this happened? How does Goldilocks look? What do you think she might be feeling?

What can you see in the picture? Which chair do you think is Mama Bear's? Why?

What do you think might be in the big blue chest?

Pages 8 and 9
Whose bed did Goldilocks jump on first? What did she say? Whose bed did she jump on next? What did she say? Whose bed did she jump on last? What did she say? What happened next?

What can you see in the picture? What are the sheets like on Papa Bear's bed? What are the sheets like on Mama Bear's bed? What are the beds made from? What shape is cut out of the headboard on Mama Bear's bed?

What is sitting on Baby Bear's bed? Do you have toys sitting on your bed? What is your bed like?

Pages 10 and 11
What did Papa Bear say when he came home? What did Mama Bear say? What did Baby Bear say?

Look at the picture. What can you see? How do the bears look? How do you think they feel?

Pages 12 and 13
What did Papa Bear say? What did Mama Bear say? What did Baby Bear say?

Look at the picture. What can you see? How does Baby Bear look? How do you think Baby Bear feels?

Pages 14 and 15
What did Papa Bear say? What did Mama Bear say? What did Baby Bear say?

Look at the picture. What can you see? How does Goldilocks look? How does Baby Bear look? What do you think Baby Bear might be feeling?

Page 16
What did Goldilocks do? Why do you think she did this? Do you think she will ever come back?

How do you think the bears feel now?

What do you think about the things that Goldilocks did? Do you think she did the right things? How might she be able to make it up to the bears?

Name

Cut out the pictures.

Put them in order to tell the story of 'Goldilocks'.

Name

Join a beginning with an ending to make sentences.
One has been done for you.

Once upon a time	Mama Bear's chair.
She tasted	and ran all the way home.
Goldilocks sat on	Baby Bear's bed.
She jumped on	there were three bears.
She jumped out of bed	Papa Bear's porridge.

Write two sentences of your own about the story.

Name

Write the correct words.

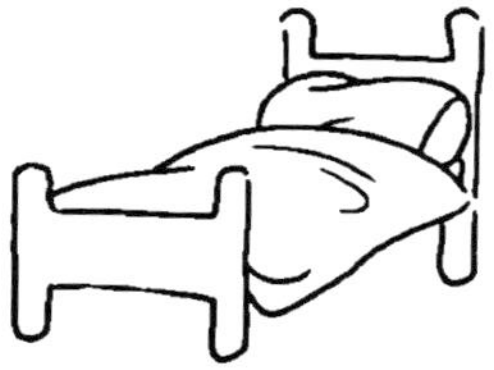

one bed

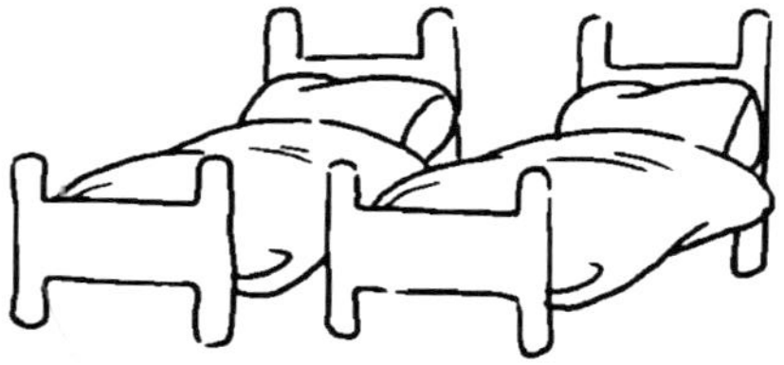

two ________

one chair

two ________

one bear

two ________

one spoon

two ________

one bowl

three _______

one book

three _______

Further activity ideas

Speaking and listening

- Talk about what the children have for breakfast. Do they have different things in winter than in summer? Who has eaten porridge? How is it made? What are their favourite breakfasts? Why? Use the discussion to talk about healthy foods and the importance of eating breakfast each day.

- Ask the children to carry out a breakfast survey of other children in the school. What is the most popular? Ask them to present their results to the rest of the class.

- Dramatise the story with the children acting the parts of the three bears and Goldilocks. Discuss the way each character might talk and how their expressions might change during different parts of the story; for example, how might the bears' faces look when they discover someone has been eating their porridge?

- Use the story to stimulate discussion about comparisons; for example, what things are tall in the classroom? What is low? What things are just right? What things are big/small/just right? What noises are loud/quiet/just right? And so on. You could turn their suggestions into a class book.

- Ask the children to bring in from home/choose from the library their favourite traditional tale. Ask them to share the book with a friend – to show them their favourite pictures and to say why they like the story.

- Ask the children to bring in their teddies. Role play a teddy bears' picnic where the children enact setting up the picnic and feeding their bears.

- Use the story to develop understanding of questions. Ask the children to invent other questions the bears could have asked, such as: Who's been in our cottage? Who's been using our spoons? Who's been sitting at our table? Who's been walking on our rug? And so on. Develop this further by asking the children to come up with three questions they could ask a friend about the story. Can their friend give or invent an answer?

Writing

- Ask the children to write another episode of the story. What happens the next day? Do the bears contact the police to arrest Goldilocks for going into their cottage? Does Goldilocks return to apologise and they all end up having a picnic together? Do the bears go to Goldilocks' house and eat her food and sit on her furniture?

- Ask the children to make a list of all the things inside the bears' house. Compare this with things inside their own homes. You could develop this into making a class picture dictionary or word bank about homes.

- Find out about real bears. What kinds are there? Where do they live? What do they eat? Make a reference book for the class or school library.

- Read other stories about bears. How many do the children know? For example, *The Teddy Robber* by Ian Beck, *My Old Teddy* by Dom Mansell and *We're Going on a Bear Hunt* by Michael Rosen. Ask the children to write their own stories about bears.

- Share other traditional tales. Ask the children to write about their favourite one. Why do they like it so much?

- Ask the children to change the ending of 'Goldilocks'. What else could have happened when she woke up to find the bears staring at her? Could the bears have asked her to live with them? Could Goldilocks help them to mend the chair and tidy up the mess she made? Could the bears have chased her into the woods where they all met a witch?

- Make plans of the bears' house. Ask the children to draw each room and label what is inside. Extend this into making plans of their own homes or the classroom.

- Have breakfast at school – include making porridge. Ask the children to write the menus.

- Go shopping for a new chair for Baby Bear! Bring in some old catalogues and ask the children to look through and make a selection of five chairs they think Baby Bear would like. They could cut out the pictures and write sentences underneath, such as 'I think Baby Bear would like this chair because...' Or the children could describe each chair or make sales flyers to send to Baby Bear.

The Three Mice by ______________________

1. Colour the picture.

Once upon a time there were three mice who lived in a teapot in the woods.

2. Colour the picture.

Every day they would go into the woods to look for food.

3. Colour the picture.

One day the mice found a cake. When they went to pick it up they saw a big cat!

4. Colour the picture.

"I am going to eat you for my dinner," the cat said.

5. Draw and write what the mice did.

6. Finish the story. Draw and write what happens in the end.

And the three miced lived happily ever after.

The Three Mice
Word bank

big	lived	spell
cake	look	teapot
cat	magic	three
day	mice	time
dinner	once	trick
eat	path	upon
every	pick	walk
food	picked	wish

My own words

8. Finish the book blurb.

This story is about a princess called Rose. Rose was very kind. She tried to make the villagers happy after a ______

____

_______________. One day Rose was captured by the _____________.

Read the story to find out what happened.

Unit 3 – Scaffold 2

1. This is the cover of your book.
   Colour it and write your name.

Princess Rose

by ______________________________

2. You are going to write a fairy tale about Princess Rose.
   Choose where she lived:
   a. a huge castle on a mountain
   b. a golden palace in a magic wood
   Draw where she lived and finish the sentence.

Once upon a time there lived a king, a queen and their daughter Princess Rose. They lived in a ______________________________ .

7. Say how the story ends. Everyone was very happy.
   The villagers were invited to:
   a. the marriage of Rose and Prince Thorn
   b. a big party
   Colour the picture and finish the sentence.

Everyone was very happy that Princess Rose was safe. They were all invited to ______________________________ .

And they all lived happily every after.

6. The king and queen asked Prince Thorn from the next kingdom to help them. He:
    a. tricked the dragon/witch
    b. killed the dragon/witch

Draw the prince helping Rose. Finish the sentence.

The king and queen asked Prince Thorn from the next kingdom to help them. Prince Thorn saved Rose by ____________

_______________________________________.

3. Choose a good beginning. Everyone in the kingdom was unhappy because:
    a. a witch had put a spell on them
    b. a big dragon lived nearby

Colour the picture and finish the sentence.

Everyone in the kingdom was very unhappy because______________________

_______________________________________.

4. Princess Rose tried to make everyone happy again by:

a. singing beautiful songs

b. playing beautiful music

Colour the picture and finish the sentence.

Princess Rose tried to make everyone feel happy again by ________________ ________________________________ .

5. Say what happened next. One day:

a. the witch took Rose away and put her in a cage

b. the dragon took Rose away to his cave

Colour the picture and finish the sentence.

One day a terrible thing happened to Rose. The __________ came and ______ ______________________________ .

Everyone was very sad.

Princess Rose
Word bank

afraid	happy	princess
beautiful	invited	queen
brave	kill	rescue
captured	king	spell
carried	kingdom	terrible
castle	magic	tricked
cottage	married	unhappy
dragon	marry	villagers
fierce	palace	wicked
happily	prince	witch

My own words

Unit 4

Playscripts

A playscript is a narrative that has been written for a dramatic performance. Playscripts usually conform to the basic conventions of storytelling but playwrights do not have the same freedom with structure as story writers have. Unlike the story writer, a playwright has few descriptive tools at his disposal; he needs to establish the characters entirely through what they say and do or by what other characters say about them. The playwright does, however, have other tools to bring the story alive; namely the sets, costumes, lighting and sound.

As with stories, the plot needs to be strong to maintain interest – the audience's attention needs to be kept. This is usually achieved by making sure the individual scenes within the play end on an exciting note. The ending of the play is vital to its success. The audience needs to be satisfied that the characters' problems and adventures have come to a satisfactory conclusion – they need a 'feel-good' factor at the end of the play.

Children need to be given practice in reading plays. They need to learn about the conventions of playscripting in order to understand which parts of the text are read aloud and which parts are written as stage directions.

Plays are divided into larger sections called 'acts' with shorter sections within them called 'scenes'. The scene setting is in italics. These are messages to the director, set designer, prop maker, costume maker and lighting and sound managers. Directions for the people who are acting the roles of the characters are given in italics inside brackets too. These tell them how to perform their lines and assist the director. The characters' names are written on the left-hand side of the page to indicate which character is speaking and/or acting. The words to be spoken are set out in lines that are underneath each other.

Children need a lot of experience in writing effective narratives before they can succeed at writing plays but simple success at Key Stage 1 can be achieved through the use of structured activities such as the scaffolds in this book. Using well-known stories such as fairy tales is another way of achieving success – the characters and plot have already been decided and it is only the dialogue that needs organising.

Playscripts

Examples of playscripts

Dilly and the Wobbly Tooth by Tony Bradman (Cambridge Reading Scheme, Cambridge University Press, 2001)

The Gingerbread Boy: Play by Vivian French (Walker Books, 2000)

We're Going on a Bear Hunt: Play by Vivian French (Walker Books, 2000)

Farmer Duck: Play by Vivian French (Walker Books, 2000)

The Three Little Pigs: Play by Vivian French (Walker Books, 2000)

Little Rabbit Foo Foo: Play by Vivian French (Walker Books, 2000)

This is the Bear: Play by Vivian French (Walker Books, 2000)

Mean Green Machine: Play by Vivian French (Walker Books, 2001)

Winnie the Witch (Plays for Young People) adapted by Anthony Clark (Oberon Books, 2001)

Hansel and Gretel: Play by Stuart Paterson (Nick Hern Books, 2000)

The Twits: Plays for Children by David Wood (Puffin, 2004)

Easy Ways to Christmas Plays by Vicki Howie (Barnabas, 1998)

The Picnic - a play about Goldilocks and the three bears

retold by Jenny Feely

Questions to ask and discussion ideas

Front cover
Read the title and the author's and illustrator's names. Do the children know what a play is? How is it different from other types of story?

What do they think will happen in the play? Ask them to retell the story of Goldilocks and the three bears.

Look at the picture. Who do they think the two characters are?

Page 2
Read out the list of characters on page 2. Discuss what a narrator is. Explain that in this play the characters' names also have a picture of each one to remind them who is speaking.

How is the list of characters different from the story they know about Goldilocks? (There are a dad and a mum in this one!) Do they think this story might be different from the one they already know?

Page 3
Point out that plays are often divided into 'scenes'. Explain what this means. Explain that the first scene is set at the bears' house.

Who was in the bear family? What were they going to do?

Look at the picture. Who can you see? What else can you see?

Pages 4 and 5
What things did the bears want to take on their picnic? What did Papa Bear suggest? What did Mama Bear want? What did Baby Bear want to take? What else did they decide to take?

What can you see in the picture? What is Papa Bear holding? What is Mama Bear holding?

Pages 6 and 7
Point out that the play has now changed to Scene Two: Goldilocks' house.

What were Goldilocks' family planning to do? What did Dad want to take? What did Mum want? What did Goldilocks want? What else did they decide to take?

Look at the picture. What does Dad look like? What is Mum wearing? What are they holding? Do you think they are looking forward to the picnic? Why?

Pages 8 and 9
Point out that Scene Three is in the forest. What kinds of things are in a forest?

Where did Baby Bear decide to sit and eat his porridge? Where are Papa and Mama Bear? What did they bring to sit on?

Who has been on a picnic? Where did you go? What did you eat? What did you do?

Pages 10 and 11
Where did Goldilocks decide to sit to eat her pancakes? Where are Dad and Mum? What things did they bring?

Pages 12 and 13
What was Baby Bear thinking? What could he smell? Where was Goldilocks? What was she thinking? What could she smell?

What do you think might happen next?

Pages 14 and 15
What did Baby Bear ask Goldilocks? What did Goldilocks ask Baby Bear? What did they do?

Which would you rather eat – the pancakes or the porridge?

Page 16
What happened in the end? Why do you think they became friends?

How different is this story from the 'Goldilocks and the Three Bears' that you already know? Why do you think the story was changed? Do you like this story? Why/why not?

Name

Cut out the pictures.
Put them in order to tell the story of 'The Picnic'.

Name

Rewrite these sentences using capital letters and full stops.

1. i hate porridge

____

2. i hate pancakes

____

3. i wish i had some porridge

____

4. i wish i had some pancakes

____

5. i love porridge

____

6. i love pancakes

____

7. i wish i could eat that porridge

____

8. i wish i could eat those pancakes

____

Finish these sentences:

I hate ______________________________

I love ______________________________

Name

Circle the words that rhyme with the one in the picture.

bear

big	pear	there	over
door	some	with	chair

tree

me	three	saw	under
too	he	school	rug

jam

ham	pram	help	good
went	jar	slam	next

dad

dog	name	man	much
bad	add	had	once

eat

meet	you	people	house
old	seat	more	feet

Write some words that rhyme with 'be'.

Further activity ideas

Speaking and listening

- Ask the children to tell you about any picnics they have been on. Where did they go? Who did they go with? What did they take? What did they eat? What did they do? Bring in a picnic basket. Ask the children to draw some pictures of food they would take on a picnic and put them inside the basket. Each day you could take out two or three items from the basket and ask the child who drew the picture to say what the food is and why they like it so much.

- Discuss how 'The Picnic' differs from the original story about Goldilocks. Which version do they prefer? Can they say why? Share other alternative fairy tales, such as *Snow White in New York* by Fiona French and *The Three Little Wolves and the Big Bad Pig* by Eugene Trivizas. Ask the children to tell their own alternative versions of well-known tales.

- Discuss the children's own food likes and dislikes. Play a game to practise asking and answering questions. Sit everyone in a circle. The teacher starts and asks the person on her left a question. This person must answer in a polite way. For example:
  Teacher: 'Would you like some apples to eat?'
  Child 1: 'Yes please. I love apples!'
  Continue with Child 1 asking the person to his left:
  Child 1: 'Would you like some fish to eat?'
  Child 2: 'No thanks. I do not like fish.'
  This game can be made more fun by inventing funny questions and answers:
  Child 2: 'Would you like some spiders to eat?'
  Child 3: 'No thanks. I only eat spiders on a Sunday!'

- The children could interview their grandparents to find out what kinds of things they did on picnics. Where did they go? What did they eat? The children may be able to bring in photographs to share.

- Play memory games, such as 'I went on a picnic and I brought a chicken leg, a ... to eat,' where each child repeats the list and adds a food choice of their own.

Writing

- Ask the children to write a menu for a 'perfect' picnic! You could relate this to lessons on healthy eating. If possible, ask the children to bring in the picnic items and have a real picnic!

- What other adventures did Goldilocks and Baby Bear get up to after they became such good friends? The children could write their own stories about the two characters. Turn them into books and make a class collection of them.

- Make a class set of picnic rules in order to discuss how to look after our environment. What should we do with unwanted wrappings and bottles, for example? What do we need to remember about farm gates/country footpaths? What things are important to remember on a beach picnic? What things do we need to keep in mind if there are animals about? Develop the rules and then go on a class picnic to reinforce them. Ask the children to write about their experience.

- Ask the children to draw and label a collection of clothing/items they could take on a beach or woodland picnic. They could work in pairs or small groups to agree one list of the ten most important things to take.

- The children could write instructions for various picnic tasks, such as 'How to make a salad sandwich' or 'How to make a Thermos flask of tea'.

- Use maps of the local area to discuss possible picnic places. The children could write and/or draw directions for how to get there from their school.

- Visit local picnic sites, such as the local playground/recreation area. Ask the children to make a list of things that could be improved. This could lead to a class letter being written to the local council with their suggestions.

- Ask the children to design and label an ideal picnic site. What kinds of things would they like to have – such as play equipment, flower beds, trees for shade, a lookout point, toilets, gas barbecues, tables and chairs?

Unit 4 – Scaffold 1

Jack and the Beanstalk by ______________________

1. Colour the pictures.

Jack

Jack's mother

giant

narrator

2. Finish the sentences.

Jack's mother asked him to go out and sell their cow. Jack sold the cow to an old man for some magic beans.

You sold our c____________for some magic beans! You silly boy!

Jack's mother threw the b______________ out of the window. Next day a big beanstalk was growing there. Jack climbed up it. He saw a big house.

I will knock on the door of that big h__________ .

The giant's wife opened the d_________. Jack was so small she didn't see him go inside. A giant came into the room, so Jack hid.

Fee Fi Fo Fum! I smell the blood of a little one!

The g__________ looked all around but couldn't see anyone so he sat down and ate his d___________ .

Wife, bring me my hen!

Jack watched the h_________ lay some golden eggs! Then the giant fell asleep.

I will grab the h_________ and run home!

Jack took the hen and r_______ out very fast. The giant ran after him. Jack climbed down the b_____________________.

Quick, mother, get the axe!

Jack chopped the beanstalk down with the a______. The giant fell down and died. The hen laid golden eggs for Jack and his mother and so they were not poor any more. They _________________________

Jack and the Beanstalk
Word bank

asleep	eggs	magic
axe	fast	man
beans	fell	mother
beanstalk	giant	poor
chopped	golden	ran
climbed	hen	rich
cow	house	sold
dinner	inside	tea
door	Jack	wife

My own words

8. Finish the book blurb.

This play is about a girl called Little Red Riding Hood who went to visit her ____________________. On the way she met a ________________.

Read the story to find out what happened.

Unit 4 – Scaffold 2

1. This is the cover of your book.
   Colour it and write your name.

Little Red Riding Hood

by ____________________

2. You are going to write a play about Little Red Riding Hood.

Draw the other characters. Colour the pictures.

Narrator

Wolf

Little Red Riding Hood

Grandma

Woodcutter

7. Say how the play ends.

Finish the sentences. Draw Little Red Riding Hood in the box.

The woodcutter grabbed the ____________ and shook him. Grandma popped out of the wolf's mouth. She was not hurt. The wolf ____________________ ____________________.

Oh thank you, woodcutter. I will never talk to strangers again!

And so Little Red Riding Hood and her grandma ____________ ____________________.

6. Finish the sentences.

Draw the missing character.

And what big teeth you have!

All the better to ______ you with!

The wolf jumped on __________ __________________ and she screamed and ______________. A woodcutter who was working outside heard her and ran into the ________________.

3. Write the beginning of the play.

Draw the missing character. Finish the sentences.

Once upon a time there lived a girl called _______________ _______________. One day she went to visit her sick grandma who lived in the woods.

I hope ___________ likes these cakes I have brought for her.

A wolf jumped out in front of _________________________ .

4. Write what Little Red Riding Hood says.

Draw the missing characters. Finish the sentences.

Where are you going with that basket of ______________?

I am ______________________ .

____

Little Red Riding Hood ran away. The wolf took a short cut to Grandma's house. He ________________ on the door.

Who's there?

5. Continue the story.

Finish the sentences. Draw the missing character.

It's me, ______________________.

The wolf jumped on __________ and ate her up! He put on her clothes and got into her bed as Little Red Riding Hood came in.

Oh Grandma, what big _______ you have!

All the better to hear you with!

Little Red Riding Hood
Word bank

after	happily	pounced
ate	hear	quickly
basket	heard	screamed
better	house	shook
brought	knocked	stranger
clothes	little	suddenly
ears	lived	teeth
eat	mouth	upon
ever	once	visit
grabbed	outside	wolf
grandma	popped	woodcutter

My own words

Unit 5

Fantasy stories

Fantasy stories are very imaginative. The writer often introduces us to other worlds that frequently contain fantastic, magical creatures and incredible settings.

Sometimes the characters in fantasy stories embark on a long journey in order to attempt a quest, visiting many lands that are quite different from traditional settings to fulfil their goal. Others, as in *The Lion, the Witch and the Wardrobe*, travel to a different land by using a portal (gateway) to move instantly from one place to another. Everyday items often provide the means of entry to the other world, such as doors, mirrors or rabbit holes. Often the character is unable to control when they travel from one world to the next and this can become a key element of the story.

When characters pass from the real world into a fantasy world, they often acquire new skills or powers. These powers are usually needed to help the inhabitants of the imaginary world solve a problem. Characters usually triumph over the forces of evil and are themselves strengthened and improved in the process.

The characters in fantasy stories are not necessarily always human – dwarves, elves, wizards and many other strange creatures are often included.

Fantasy stories for older children or adults can be very lengthy tomes, often borrowing themes from ancient myths and traditional epics. They are usually very descriptive in style and as a result the author is able to create and populate fictional worlds that have little or no bearing on reality. These stories tend to lend themselves to being written in a series.

Fantasy stories for young children tend to restrict themselves to the simpler elements of the genre – fantastic creatures, an element of magic and a journey to a different place. In this respect they can be very similar to fairy tales but they usually lack the traditional characters, such as the king, queen, princess and prince, and traditional settings, such as the castle, village and cottage.

Fantasy stories

Examples of fantasy stories

The Dragon Machine by Helen Ward (Templar, 2003)

The Magic Finger by Roald Dahl (Puffin, 2001)

The Troublesome Tooth Fairy by Sandi Toksvig (Corgi Pups, 2000)

The Other Ark by Lynley Dodd (Puffin, 2005)

The Magic Paintbrush by Julia Donaldson (Macmillan Children's, 2004)

The Worst Witch by Jill Murphy (Puffin, 2004)

Through the Magic Mirror by Anthony Browne (Walker Books, 2001)

Seven Ways to Catch the Moon by M P Robertson (Frances Lincoln, 2000)

Annie and the Pirates

by Jenny Feely

Questions to ask and discussion ideas

Front cover
Read the title and the author's and illustrator's names. What is a pirate? What other stories do you know with pirates in them?

Look at the picture. What can you see? Do the pirates look friendly? What do you think might happen in the story?

Pages 2 and 3
Look at the picture. What buildings can you see? Is the town old or new?

What are the pirates wearing? Why do you think they have swords?

The pirates found a box, a bag and a girl called Annie. Can you see these things in the picture? What do you think might be inside the box? What might be in the bag? What do you think the pirates might do with these things? Where do you think they will take Annie?

Pages 4 and 5
Who did the pirates meet back on the ship? Was he pleased with what the pirates brought back? What did he want them to bring him? What kinds of things do you think would be counted as treasure?

Why was Annie frightened? What plan do you think she might have?

Pages 6 and 7
What did Annie tell the pirates? How do you think she might use a feather and an empty box to fight a sea monster?

What might a sea monster look like?

Pages 8 and 9
Why do you think the Pirate King changed his mind about throwing the box and the feather away?

Look at the picture. It shows what the Pirate King thinks the sea monster looks like. How big is the monster? What colour is it? What might it do to the ship?

Pages 10 and 11
What happened to the sea in the night? What appeared from the depths of the sea? What was it covered in?

What did the sea monster do? What did the Pirate King do? What did he hold onto? How do you think he feels? What do you think might happen next?

What would you do if you were the Pirate King?

Pages 12 and 13
What did Annie do? What did the monster do?

What happened as the monster began to laugh? What did Annie do next?

What kind of jewels do you think they were?

What do you think the sea monster will do now?

Pages 14 and 15
What did the sea monster do when Annie stopped tickling him? Why do you think he was never seen again? What do you think might have happened to him?

How do you think the Pirate King felt? What did the Pirate King ask Annie to do? Why do you think he asked her this?

What did Annie reply? Why do you think she said this?

Page 16
What happened in the end? What do you think Annie will do with the box and the feather?

What do you think the pirates will do next?

Name

Cut out the pictures.
Put them in order to tell the story of 'Annie and the Pirates'.

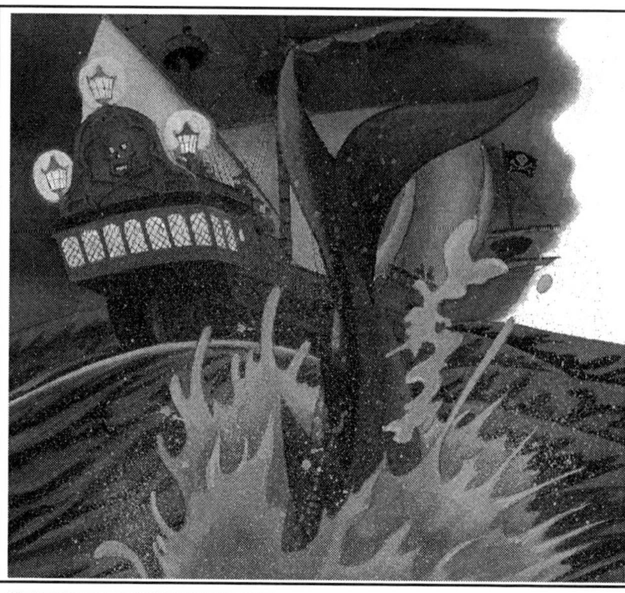

Name

Circle all the words that are about pirates.
Write them in the treasure chest.

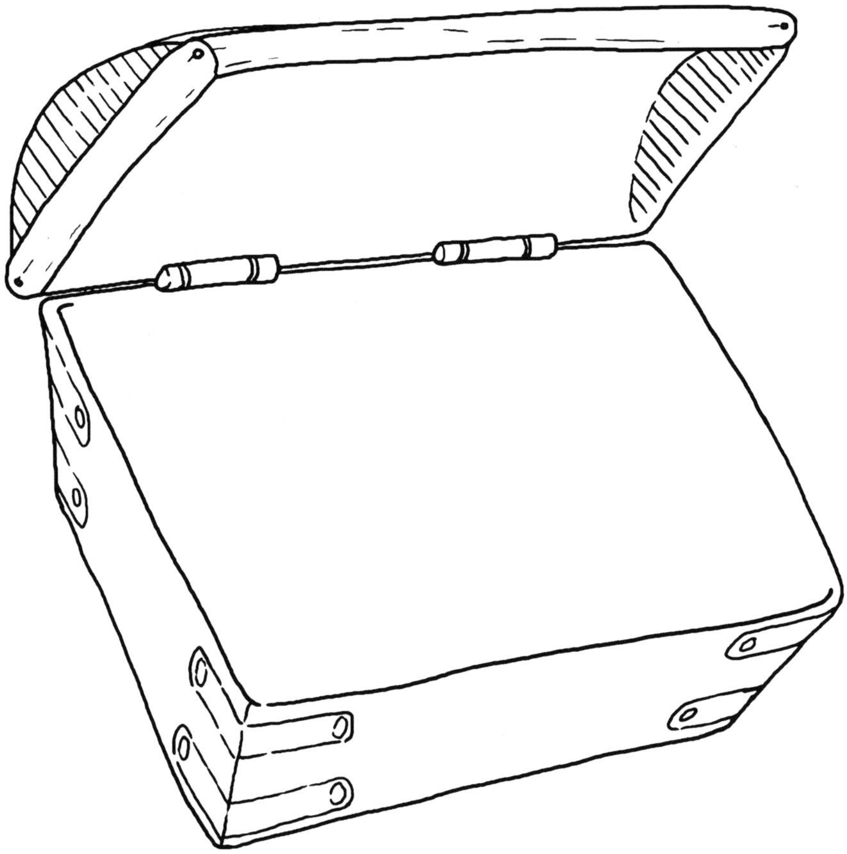

ship	good
dog	bad
parrot	sister
house	sea
school	sailed
treasure	fight
deck	time

Use words from the treasure chest to finish the sentences.

1. The ship ________________ on the sea.

2. The pirates were looking for ____________________.

3. The pirates stood on the __________ of the ship.

4. One of the pirates had a pet ______________.

5. Sometimes pirates ______________ other people.

6. The pirate _____________ has sails.

Name

Add 'ed' to these words.
The first one has been done for you.

look	looked	sail	______________
call	______________	jump	______________
peep	______________	roar	______________
reach	______________	splash	______________
ask ______________		laugh	______________

Use these words in a sentence.

1. jumped

____

2. sailed

____

3. asked

____

4. splashed

____

Further activity ideas

Speaking and listening

- ❑ Ask the children to tell you what they already know about pirates. What do they usually look like? What do they wear? What do they do? Ask them to tell you about any other pirate stories they have heard or read. How might a pirate speak and behave? Ask the children to pretend to be pirates. They could act out the following:
  - looking through a telescope
  - digging for treasure
  - fighting with their cutlass
  - walking the plank
  - scrubbing the deck
  - setting the sails.

  What might they say as they do these things? Invent some catchphrases.

- ❑ Talk about how important it is to navigate a ship so it doesn't hit any rocks or other ships. Set up an obstacle course with furniture/PE equipment as potential risks to a ship, such as a reef, a lighthouse on a rocky outcrop, a tanker and so on. Ask the children to work in pairs – one to be the ship, the other to be the navigator. Challenge the navigator to call out directions to the 'ship' in order to navigate the obstacle course safely. (For example, 'Take three steps forward. Turn to the right. Take four steps...')

- ❑ Play memory games, such as 'I found a treasure chest and inside it was a...' where each person in the circle has to add another item to the chest. Can the next person remember all the items?

- ❑ Ask the children to work in pairs to think of a different ending to the story. Does the sea monster take Annie away rather than laughing and spilling the jewels? Does the Pirate King fight the sea monster instead? Bring the class back together and share their ideas. How many different endings were invented? Which one do they like best? Why?

- ❑ Ask the children to use musical instruments to make sounds for different parts of the story – such as the waves crashing on the shore, the pirates walking on the deck, the monster splashing in the sea, the monster roaring or laughing, the jewels falling on the deck. Ask the others to listen to the sounds. Can they guess what they are?

- ❑ Make a treasure chest from a box. Cover it in sparkly paper. Ask the children to draw and label an item that they really treasure. It could be their favourite toy or person. Each day select a treasure from the box and ask that child to say why they treasure it so much.

Writing

- ❑ What other adventures did the pirates get up to? Ask the children to write their own stories about the pirates.

- ❑ Find out about pirates. Make a class book with the children's writing and drawings for everyone to share.

- ❑ Ask the children to draw and label treasure maps. Can they write instructions for how to find the treasure?

- ❑ 'Bury' some treasure in the classroom or playground. Over the course of a week give written instructions to small groups of children to follow. Can they find the treasure?

- ❑ Ask the children to invent a sea monster of their own. They could draw and describe it, then write sentences or a story about it.

- ❑ Create a word wall of sea words. Use the words to make sea rhymes and poems.

- ❑ Create a counting rhyme about sea monsters or pirates. For example:

  one sea monster swam in the sea
  two sea monsters had a cup of tea

  three sea monsters chased my ship
  four sea monsters gave me a nip

  five sea monsters ate my cake
  six sea monsters swam in the lake

- ❑ Discuss why the sea monster was never seen again. Where did he go? What happened to him? Ask the children to write a story about what happened to the sea monster.

- ❑ Draw a ship or treasure chest shape and photocopy it. Ask the children to use dictionaries and other sources to find as many words as they can that begin with 'sh' or 'tr'. They can write them inside the shape for display.

The Land of the Dragons by ______________________

1. Colour the picture.

Cassy was looking in the loft.
She found an old book.

2. Colour the picture.

When she opened the book a dragon popped out in a puff of smoke.

3. Draw Cassy on the dragon's back and colour the picture.

'I need your help,' said the dragon. 'Climb on my back.
I will take you to my land.'
The dragon took her to a big castle. They met an old wizard.

4. Colour the picture.

He told her that he had dropped his magic wand down a hole. No-one was small enough to get it out.

5. Draw and write about what Cassy does.

6. Finish the story. Draw and write what happens in the end.

The Land of the Dragons
Word bank

attic
book
boxes
castle
climbed
dragon
dropped
fly
flying

happy
help
home
land
magic
picked
returned
rope
safely

small
wand
wizard

My own words

8. Finish the book blurb.

This story is about a boy called Jansen who finds himself in a different world. He meets a ____________________ who needs his help. Together they __________

__________________________________.

Read the story to find out what happened.

Unit 5 – Scaffold 2

1. This is the cover of your book.
Colour it and write your name.

Jansen's magic trip

by ______________________________

2. You are going to write a story about a boy called Jansen who travels to another land. Choose how he gets there:
   a. through a magic mirror
   b. through a magic book

Colour the picture and finish the sentence.

One day Jansen was holding his new ____________ when he suddenly found himself in a strange forest!

7. Say how the story ends. Jansen got the item back. The wizard was so pleased he:
   a. gave Jansen a hundred gold coins
   b. made Jansen into a junior wizard

Draw Jansen and the wizard. Finish the sentences.

Jansen used the __________ to help him get the ______________________ back.
The wizard was so happy he __________ ________________________________ .

6. Say how they travelled to this place. Inca got all his friends and they:
   a. rode on the backs of giant elephants
   b. sat on magic flying carpets

   Draw a picture of their journey. Finish the sentence.

Inca called to all his friends and together they went to the place on ______________ ______________________________________ .

3. Choose a good beginning. Jansen met:
   a. a goblin called Inca who lived in a log hut
   b. a tiny dragon called Inca who lived in a cave

   Draw a picture of Jansen and Inca and finish the sentence.

Jansen saw a path in the forest. After he had walked for a while he met a ________________ called ____________ who lived in a _________________________.

4. Inca told Jansen that he needed his help to find the wizard's:

   a. book of spells that had been lost

   b. magic lamp that had been stolen

Colour the picture and finish the sentence.

Inca told Jansen that he needed his help to ______________________________ .

5. Say what happened next. Jansen knew what to do. He:

   a. looked into his mirror and could see where it was

   b. opened his book and a magic map showed him where it was

Draw a picture of Jansen and finish the sentence.

Jansen knew what to do. He ______________________________ .

Jansen's magic trip
Word bank

appeared	help	spells
bedroom	hundred	suddenly
carpets	journey	tiny
elephants	lamp	travel
flying	magic	travelled
forest	mirror	walked
friends	pathway	wizard
giant	pleased	
happy	quickly	

My own words

Unit 6

Animal stories

Animal stories are one of the most popular types of story for children. The popularity of this genre can often be attributed to the authors' use of anthropomorphism where the animal characters within the story are given human feelings, characteristics and behaviour. This allows the reader to identify more closely with the animal characters, enabling him to appreciate their problems and situations more sympathetically.

Many animal stories have been written to teach a moral lesson as well as to entertain. Children, it seems, are more willing to accept a moral 'lecture' from a cute animal character than from a human one!

There are different types of animal stories:

- realistic ones where the animals behave as they would do in the wild (such as the ponies in the 'Sheltie' series of books by Peter Clover);
- stories with fantasy animals in them (such as *The Gruffalo* by Julia Donaldson);
- anthropomorphic stories (such as *Fantastic Mr Fox* by Roald Dahl);
- stories with humans and animals in them (such as *Farmer Duck* by Martin Waddell);
- stories with only animals in them (such as *Elmer* by David McKee).

The anthropomorphic aspect of animal stories allows the author to deal with more challenging storylines for children than in conventional stories about humans. The reader is more willing to accept the harsh truths of issues such as separation and death (such as *Old Pig* by Margaret Wild) or being scared (such as *Let's Go Home, Little Bear* by Martin Waddell) if they are presented in stories about animals.

Friendships too can be more unconventional in animal stories, such as between Eeyore, Piglet and Tigger in the 'Winnie the Pooh' books by A A Milne.

Although the characters may have human characteristics, most animal stories also make sure the characters have specific animal traits such as the dogs in *101 Dalmations* by Dodie Smith.

Animal stories

Examples of animal stories

Russell the Sheep by Rob Scotton (HarperCollins, 2005)

Mrs McTats and Her Houseful of Cats by Alyssa Satin Capucilli (Simon & Schuster, 2003)

Owl Babies by Martin Waddell (Walker Books, 1994)

The Snail and the Whale by Julia Donaldson (Macmillan, 2003)

Percy the Park Keeper: A Classic Treasury by Nick Butterworth (HarperCollins, 2006)

The Story of the Little Mole by Werner Holzwarth (David Bennett Books, 1994)

Six Dinner Sid by Inga Moore (Simon & Schuster, 1991)

Lizard's Tail

by Mark Gagiero

Questions to ask and discussion ideas

Front cover
Read the title and the author's and illustrator's names.

Look at the picture. What does the lizard look like? Where do lizards live? What do they eat? Who has seen a lizard? Where?

What might the story be about? What might happen to the lizard's tail?

Page 2
What did the lizard ask the peacock? What did the peacock reply?

What do you think may have happened to the lizard's tail? What is special about a peacock?

Why do Peacock and Lizard have a capital initial letter?

Page 3
Where did Lizard go? What kind of tail did she see? Who do you think the tail belongs to?

What else can you see in the picture?

Page 4
Who did the tail belong to? What did Lizard ask Dog? What did Dog reply?

What does Dog look like? What other kinds of dogs do you know?

Page 5
What kind of tail did Lizard see in the tree? Who do you think it belongs to?

Page 6
Who did the tail belong to? What kind of creature is a possum? Why do you think he lives in a hole in a tree? Do they live in our country?

What did Lizard ask Possum? What did Possum reply?

Page 7
Where did Lizard go? What kind of tail did she see? Who do you think it belongs to?

Page 8
Who did the tail belong to? What colour was Mouse?

What did Lizard ask Mouse? What did Mouse reply? Why do you think Mouse lives in a hole in the bank?

Page 9
Where did Lizard go? What kind of tail did she see? Who do you think the tail belongs to?

Page 10
Who did the tail belong to? What does Monkey look like? Where do monkeys live? What sorts of things do they do?

What did Lizard ask Monkey? What did Monkey reply?

Page 11
Where did Lizard go? What kind of tail did she see? Who do you think it belongs to?

Page 12
Who did the tail belong to? What did Lizard ask Snake? What did Snake reply?

Have you ever seen a snake? What do you know about snakes?

Page 13
Who did Lizard go to see? Where did Owl live? What does Owl look like?

Page 14
What did Lizard ask? Where were all the places Lizard had looked for her tail?

What do you think Owl might say?

Page 15
What did Owl reply? How does Lizard look? Where do you think her tail is?

Page 16
What had happened to Lizard's tail? How do you think Lizard feels now? Did you know that a lizard's tail can grow back after it has broken off?

Name all the animals in the story. How many of these live in our country?

What did you like best about this story?

Name

Cut out the pictures.
Put them in order to tell the story of 'Lizard's Tail'.

Name

Put a **?** at the end of these sentences.

1. Have you seen my tail
2. Why did Lizard lose her tail
3. Where do lizards live
4. What colour was Monkey

Finish these sentences. Don't forget the **?**

1. Where was Lizard's _______________
2. Did Possum live in a hole in a _____________
3. Why was Lizard so _______________
4. Why do snakes live in the _______________

Now write four questions that you could ask Lizard.

1. ____
2. ____
3. ____
4. ____

Name

Names should start with a capital letter.
Circle all the names in the box below.
Write them below with a capital letter.

tom	under	sally	peter	door
tree	ahmed	table	window	andrew
cup	james	house	sharon	school

Rewrite these sentences, putting in the capital letters.

1. sam and michael went to the park.

2. On Monday sunil and sanjeet went swimming.

3. Today is claire's birthday. She is five.

4. My brother, paul, is going to ben's house for tea.

Write the names of all the people in your family.

Further activity ideas

Speaking and listening

- Ask the children to tell you what they already know about lizards. What kind of animal are they? What do they look like? Where do they live? What do they eat? Provide small groups of children with information books about lizards. Ask them to find out two new things about lizards. Ask each group to tell the others what they found out. Make the information into a class book.

- Ask the children to tell a friend about their favourite animal and why they like it so much. Come together as a class to share their ideas. Is there a class favourite?

- Perform the book as a play with the children acting the animal parts and the teacher as narrator.

- Pretend to be animals! Ask the children to make the noises and movements of animals. Can others guess what they are from the sound alone? From the movement alone?

- The children could tell others about animal incidents from their own experiences – 'My first pet', 'The day our dog escaped', 'My uncle's farm', 'How I care for my fish' and so on.

- Ask one child to think of an animal. The others ask questions to which the answer can only be 'Yes' or 'No', such as 'Is it a mammal?', and try to guess what it is.

- Set up a role play area that features animals, such as a farm, a veterinary clinic or a pet shop.

- Share other stories about animals. Ask the children to bring in their favourite animal book from home or the school library and ask them to tell others why they like it.

- Have fun with well-known animal stories by asking the children to replace the animal's name each time with the animal's sound. For example, 'Once upon a time there lived three little "oink, oinks". The first little "oink, oink" lived in a house made of sticks...'

Writing

- Make an ABC of animals. Provide the children with information books/dictionaries and ask them to make lists of animals for each letter of the alphabet.

- Give the children magazines with pictures of animals in them. Ask them to cut out the pictures. They could glue two pictures onto a blank piece of paper and write speech bubbles for what the animals might be saying to each other.

- Make instruction books on how to care for class or home pets.

- Ask a vet or member of the RSPCA to visit the class. Ask the children to prepare some questions to ask about animal care. Each child could write their question and the answer in a class book – together with drawings/cuttings from magazines.

- Ask the children to invent a fantasy animal! They could create a new creature by cutting out the heads, legs, tails and bodies of various animals from magazines and recombining them in different ways or drawing their own. Ask them to write a description of the animals – where it lives, what it eats, what it does during the day and so on.

- Create alliterative animal counting rhymes, such as:

  one orange owlet
  two terrific tortoises
  three thrilling thrushes
  four fancy fish
  five fast foxes
  six slithering snakes
  seven sleepy squirrels
  eight enormous elephants
  nine noisy nanny goats
  ten tiny tadpoles

- Invent a zoo! Ask the children to draw and label a map of an imaginary zoo. They can add pictures and descriptions of all the animals in their zoo. They could create a handbook for the zookeeper, a visitors' guide and advertisements to promote the zoo.

Pippa's Bone by ______________________

1. Colour the picture.

Pippa loved her toy bone. She took it everywhere with her. She took it on her walk.

2. Colour the picture.

She played with it in the garden. She took it to bed with her.

3. Colour the picture.

But one day her bone was gone! Pippa looked everywhere for it. She looked in the house. She looked in the garden.

4. Colour the picture.

She looked in her bed. But she did not find it. Pippa was very sad.

5. Draw and write what Pippa does.

6. Finish the story. Draw and write what happens in the end.

Pippa's Bone
Word bank

bed	found	sad
behind	garden	toy
bone	happy	under
chew	house	very
chewed	inside	walk
dinner	look	woke
dog	looked	
everywhere	outside	
find	played	

My own words

Unit 6 – Scaffold 2

8. Finish the book blurb.

This story is about a duck called Thomas and a dog called Bounce. They loved to play in their pond but one day ________

____

____.

Read the story to find out what happened.

1. This is the cover of your book. Colour it and write your name.

Thomas and Bounce

by ________________________

2. You are going to write a story about a duck called Thomas and a dog called Bounce. Choose where they lived:

   a. on a farm in the country

   b. in a big garden in the town

   Colour the picture and finish the sentence.

Thomas the duck and Bounce the dog lived together. They lived ______________________________________ .

7. Say how the story ends. Thomas and Bounce were very happy because:

   a. they could share their new pond with all their friends

   b. they set up a swimming club and made lots of money

   Colour the picture. Finish the sentence.

Thomas and Bounce were very happy with their new pond. They ______________________________________ .

6. Say how the problem was solved. Thomas and Bounce:
    a. asked their owners to create a new pond
    b. asked their friends to dig a much bigger pond and got the fire brigade to fill it

Draw a picture of the new pond. Finish the sentence.

Thomas and Bounce had an idea. They decided to________________________

____

____

____

3. Choose a good beginning. Thomas and Bounce were best friends. Choose what they liked to do:
    a. play tug of war with Bounce's lead
    b. chase each other around the roses

Draw a picture of the two friends and finish the sentences.

Thomas and Bounce were best

________________ .

They liked to ______________________ .

4. Say what they liked doing best. In the pond they:

   a. paddled in the water and got very wet

   b. squelched in the mud and got very dirty

Draw a picture of Thomas and Bounce and finish the sentences.

Thomas and Bounce liked playing in the ____________ best. They ____________

____

________________________________.

5. Give them a problem. The pond had gone because:

   a. it was very hot and it had dried up

   b. someone had filled it in to make a flower garden

Colour the picture and finish the sentence.

One day a bad thing happened. Their lovely pond had ____________ because

____

________________________________.

Thomas and Bounce were very ________.

Thomas and Bounce
Word bank

because	fire brigade	owners
build	flower	paddled
business	friends	playing
chase	garden	pond
country	happened	sad
decided	happy	squelch
dirty	idea	swimming pool
dried	lovely	terrible
farm	money	town

My own words